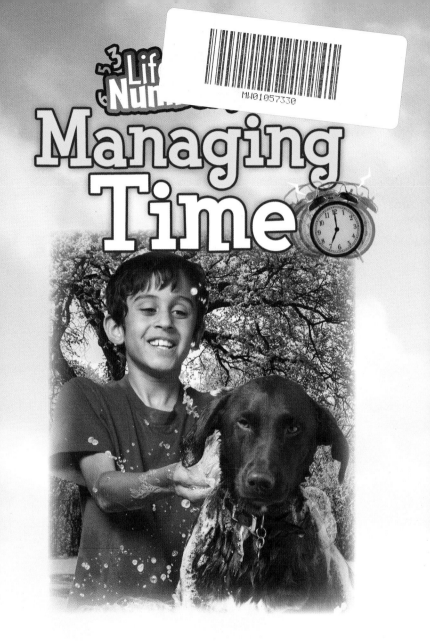

Life in Numbers
Managing Time

Lisa Perlman Greathouse

Publishing Credits

Rachelle Cracchiolo, M.S.Ed., *Publisher*
Conni Medina, M.A.Ed., *Managing Editor*
Nika Fabienke, Ed.D., *Series Developer*
June Kikuchi, *Content Director*
John Leach, *Assistant Editor*
Lee Aucoin, *Senior Graphic Designer*

TIME For Kids and the TIME For Kids logo are registered trademarks of TIME Inc. Used under license.

Image Credits: Cover and p.1 RubberBall/Alamy Stock Photo; pp.8–9 Macduff Everton/Getty Images; p.15 (inset) Bill Ray/Life Magazine/ The LIFE Premium Collection/Getty Images, (full page) Nickolas Muray/ George Eastman House/Getty Images; all other images from iStock and/ or Shutterstock

Teacher Created Materials
5301 Oceanus Drive
Huntington Beach, CA 92649-1030
http://www.tcmpub.com
ISBN 978-1-4258-4969-6
© 2018 Teacher Created Materials, Inc.

Table of Contents

What Did You Do Today?

Are you having a good day? (I hope so!) Think about everything you have done since you woke up. Did you brush your teeth and eat breakfast? How did you get to school? Did you walk or take a bus? Or did somebody drive you?

Going Deeper

Now, let's think about other things you probably did today. Did you look at a computer, cell phone, or television? Did you read a book? (You've started at least one!) There are people who study how we spend our time. They use that information to help learn about people and **society**.

4

Time Before Clocks?

Before there were clocks, people watched the sun and the moon for clues about time. In the 1300s, the **mechanical** clock was developed. It measures time with gears and weights.

Wait a Minute!

Do you know how many minutes are in a day? We know there are 24 hours in a day and 60 minutes in each hour.

24 hours	×	60 minutes	=	1440
per day		per hour		minutes per day

Your Daily Schedule

You likely spend more time sleeping than doing any other activity. People sleep a lot. In fact, people spend one-third of their lives asleep!

Sleeping Like a Baby

When you were a baby, you slept almost twice as much as you do now. Newborns sleep about 16 hours every day! But they still wake up every 2 to 4 hours—even during the night. That's why new parents are tired all the time! You should try to get 9 to 11 hours of sleep. When you are well rested, your body is ready to take on the day!

Why Grandpa Likes His Naps

Does it seem as if your grandparents sleep a lot? As we get older, we don't sleep as **soundly** as we did when we were younger. That's why many older people take naps during the day.

Can You "Catch" a Yawn?

Does looking at this cat make you want to yawn? Everyone yawns—even animals. But experts haven't figured out why seeing a yawn makes you want to do it, too!

If you sleep 10 hours each night, you're left with 14 hours in your day. You probably spend about half of that time learning!

Time for School!

Most kids in the United States spend 6 or 7 hours a day in school. Most of those hours are spent in class. But some time is spent eating lunch (and maybe breakfast, too) and at recess. You probably spend part of the school day talking to friends. Hopefully, that's only during lunch and recess!

School Hours

How much time you spend in school depends on where you live. Children in Chile spend 1,007 hours in school each year. In Russia, students spend just 470 hours.

Homework Counts!

Teens in the United States spend about 6 hours a week doing homework. In China, it's closer to 14 hours. But in Finland, it is only 3.

0|6
hours per week

classroom in Chile

9

Get to Work!

What are the grown-ups in your life doing while you are in school?

Many adults spend about 8 hours at work. That's one-third of a day! Some people work during the day. Others, such as nurses and police officers, may work at night and on weekends. Some people commute far distances to get to work. Others are able to use a computer to work at home.

High Achievers

Many high school and college students work *and* go to school. That doesn't leave much time for fun. But they know that all their hard work will help them reach their goals!

Work, Work, Work

People in the United States work a lot. They work about 71 more hours every year than people in Japan. They work 308 more hours each year than people in France. That's a lot of work!

Getting There Is Half the Fun

In big cities, people spend a lot of time getting to work and school. They may take trains or buses instead of driving. They may even carpool to school!

11

Let's Play

Here's where things get fun. After school, your time is spent doing things you like!

What's your favorite thing to do? Do you like to play soccer? Do you like to bake cookies? Do you play video games with friends? Do you draw or read? Maybe you like riding bicycles with friends. We all enjoy different kinds of activities. The time you spend doing things just for fun is called *leisure time*. Almost 96 percent of people have 5 hours a day of leisure time. That's almost one-fifth of an entire day—although it probably seems like leisure time just flies by!

Screen Time

Kids ages 9 to 11 log more than 4 hours of screen time each day. That includes TV, video games, and social media. How much time do you spend looking at a screen each day?

0 4
hours per day

LOL!

Many people spend part of their days laughing—and the younger you are, the more you laugh. Young children typically laugh 10 times more than adults.

Fun for Grandparents

Have you ever wondered what your grandparents did for fun when they were your age? They didn't have cell phones or laptops. There were just a few TV channels to choose from. There was no Internet. And no one had invented video games!

Jigsaw puzzles and games such as **jacks** and marbles used to be very popular. So were roller-skating and board games. Ask your grandparents about their favorite games when they were young. If you played them now, you would probably think they are fun, too!

kids doing a jigsaw puzzle

Not Just a Hoop

In 1958, Wham-O® Toys sold hoops made out of a plastic tube. It was called the Hula Hoop®. Soon, more than 25 million hoops were spinning around people's waists!

LIFE

The 50s

WACKY REVIVAL OF
Hula hoops
Ducktails
Sock hops
Marilyn Monroe
Rock 'n' roll
Elvis himself
plus a 50s q

Time for Chores

Now that we've had our fun, it's time for chores! When we're part of a family, we all need to pitch in to make sure things get done.

Do you make your bed in the morning and put your dirty clothes in the hamper? Feed the dog? Take out the trash? It's not always fun, but helping out around the house is a good way to learn responsibility. If you help out without being asked, that's even better. The other members of your family will appreciate it!

More Chores

Chores for grown-ups include cooking and cleaning. Women spend about $2\frac{1}{2}$ hours doing chores most days. Men spend closer to 2 hours on chores.

Time to Pitch In!

Kids in the United States spend an **average** of 3 hours per week on housework. Compare that to almost 28 hours per week watching TV! Next time you get ready to watch a show, think about whether there's a chore you should take care of first!

0:3 hours per week

Time for Essentials

Do you ever think about what you can do to help others? Have you ever picked up trash at a park? Maybe you carried in grocery bags for an older neighbor. These are things we do to be good citizens. We can make the world a better place. It's called **volunteering**. About 25 percent of people in the United States volunteer.

There are many types of volunteering. People donate food and work in soup kitchens. People clean neighborhoods and plant trees. Helping others makes people feel good!

Just One Day

Mark Make A Difference Day® on your calendar. It happens once a year. People volunteer on the fourth Saturday in October. Can you think of a way to help others on this day?

The Best Gift of All

Do you love animals? Help your local shelter. For your birthday, ask friends to bring pet supplies instead of gifts. Giving can be the best gift of all!

Getting Hungry?

Most of us enjoy a good meal. How much time do people spend eating each day?

We spend about 67 minutes a day eating. That's about twice as long as we spend each day making our food. With fast food and frozen food, our meals are ready a lot faster than in the past. Experts say we should all be eating more fruits and vegetables. They hardly take any time to prepare!

Meal Times

In certain parts of the world, people eat only two or three times a day. They rarely snack. In France, lunch is the biggest meal of the day, and it may have many courses—even in school cafeterias!

Mountain-Top Brownies

Did you know baking takes less time in higher places? Imagine you start baking brownies at your house near the beach. At the same time, your friend starts baking at his house in the mountains. Your brownies will take about 30 minutes. Your friend's will only take 20 minutes.

Get Ready!

"When will you be out of the bathroom?" If you share a bathroom at home, you probably ask that question many times each day. It can be frustrating. People can take a long time to get ready.

Think about all the things you do in the bathroom every day. You brush your teeth. You shower or take a bath. You dry and brush your hair. You use the toilet. These all fall under the term "personal care." Grown-ups spend more time getting ready than kids do. This is because there is more personal care to do when you get older, such as shaving or putting on makeup.

Sing While You Wash

You know that you should wash your hands often. But did you know that you should soap up for 20 seconds before rinsing? Sing the "Happy Birthday" song twice to know when time's up!

Prep Time

How much time do you spend getting ready each morning? Does it take you 30 minutes every day? Think about how much total time that would be for one whole year. That's 7 days!

30 minutes per day

23

Pay Attention!

Does your mind wander at times during the day? This is called daydreaming. And it turns out that we spend quite a bit of time doing it.

You might look out the window while someone is talking to you. All of a sudden, you are not listening. Your mind wanders. You might be thinking about what is for dinner. People spend almost half of their time thinking about something other than what they are doing. In small amounts, daydreaming can make us more creative. But it can become a problem if you do it too often—like at school!

Ready, Set, Daydream!

The average daydream does not take long. It lasts just 14 seconds!

24

Dream or Real?

Do you ever have dreams that seem so real that you wake up and think they are? We spend more than 2 hours dreaming every night. But we don't always remember our dreams the next day.

0 2
hours per night

Every Moment Counts

Now you know how people spend their time. Can you think of ways to get even more out of your day?

Each morning, take a few seconds to think about something you're grateful for. Is it your family? A friend? Your pet? It's a great way to start your day with a positive attitude. Think about other ways to make the most of your day. Help out at home by making your lunch. Offer to do homework with a friend who is struggling. Pick up a piece of trash instead of walking by it. Every day you have a new opportunity to make the world a better place!

The Time of Our Lives

How long you live depends on where you live. People in Japan live about 83.7 years. This is the longest of any country. More than 65,000 people who are more than 100 years old live in Japan!

Glossary

average—a number you get by adding quantities and then dividing the total by the number of things

jacks—a game in which small metal objects with six points are picked up while bouncing and catching a ball

jigsaw puzzles—pictures that are formed from small pieces that fit together

mechanical—related to machines

society—the people of a particular area at a particular time

soundly—deeply and without interruption

volunteering—doing something to help others without being asked

Index

Check It Out!

Books

Skurzynski, Gloria. 2000. *On Time.* National Geographic Society.

Websites

The Atlantic. *Your Day in a Chart: 10 Cool Facts About How Americans Spend Our Time.* www.theatlantic.com.

Grandparents.com. *Favorite Pastimes, Revisited: 10 Retro Activities to Share With Kids.* www.grandparents.com.

Make a Difference Day. www.makeadifferenceday.com.

Try It!

Create a calendar that shows how you spend your time every day for a week. Pick 5 activities that you want to track. They can be things like sleeping, school, TV, computer, and eating. Keep track of how many hours you spend doing each activity.

Do any of the numbers surprise you? How might you change your habits to better balance your day?

	M	T	W	Th	F	Sat	Sun
Sleeping	9	$8\frac{1}{2}$					
School	6	6					
TV	$2\frac{1}{2}$	$2\frac{1}{2}$					
Computer	1	1					
Eating	$2\frac{1}{2}$	2					

About the Author

Lisa Perlman Greathouse grew up in Brooklyn, New York. She has loved writing since she was in elementary school. She wrote for her high school and college newspapers. She became a journalist after she finished school. Today, she works at Disney. She and her husband have two grown children and live in Southern California.